The Love Letters of Phyllis McGinley

The Love Letters

of

Phyllis McGinley

New York · The Viking Press · 1954

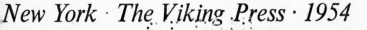

Copyright 1951, 1952, 1953, 1954 by Phyllis McGinley
Published by The Viking Press in September 1954
Published on the same day in the Dominion of Canada
by The Macmillan Company of Canada Limited
Second Printing September 1954
Third Printing October 1954

Grateful acknowledgment is made to *The New Yorker*,
in which the majority of these poems originally ap-
peared; also to *The Atlantic, Good Housekeeping,
The Griffin, Harper's Magazine, Mademoiselle, Har-
per's Bazaar, America,* and *The New York Times.*

Library of Congress catalog number: 54-9882

Printed in U.S.A. by the Vail-Ballou Press, Inc.

For Julie

who ungrudgingly sat for her portrait

Contents

The Love Letters of Phyllis McGinley

Apologia

When I and the world
Were greener and fitter,
Many a bitter
Stone I hurled.
Many a curse
I used to pitch
At the universe,
Being so rich
I had goods to spare;
Could afford to notice
The blight on the lotus,
The worm in the pear.

But needier grown
(If little wiser)
Now, like a miser,
All that I own
I celebrate
Shamefacedly—
The pear on my plate,
The fruit on my tree,
Though sour and small;
Give, willy-nilly,
Thanks for the lily,
Spot and all.

A LITTLE PRAISE

Though a seeker since my birth,
Here is all I've learned on earth,
This the gist of what I know:
Give advice and buy a foe.
Random truths are all I find
Stuck like burs about my mind.
Salve a blister. Burn a letter.
Do not wash a cashmere sweater.
Tell a tale but seldom twice.
Give a stone before advice.

Pressed for rules and verities,
All I recollect are these:
Feed a cold to starve a fever.
Argue with no true believer.
Think-too-long is never-act.
Scratch a myth and find a fact.
Stitch in time saves twenty stitches.
Give the rich, to please them, riches.
Give to love your hearth and hall.
But do not give advice at all.

Love Note to a Playwright

Perhaps the literary man
    I most admire among my betters
Is Richard Brinsley Sheridan,
    Who, viewing life as more than letters,
Persisted, like a stubborn Gael,
In not acknowledging his mail.

They say he hardly ever penned
    A proper "Yrs. received & noted,"
But spent what time he had to spend
    Shaping the law that England voted,
Or calling, on his comic flute,
The tune for Captain Absolute.

Though chief of the prodigious wits
    That Georgian taverns set to bubblin',
He did not answer Please Remits
    Or scoldings from his aunts in Dublin
Or birthday messages or half
The notes that begged an autograph.

I hear it sent his household wild—
    Became a sort of parlor fable—
The way that correspondence piled,
    Mountainous, on his writing table,
While he ignored the double ring
And wouldn't answer *any*thing;

Not scrawls from friends or screeds from foes
    Or scribble from the quibble-lover
Or chits beginning "I enclose
    Manuscript under separate cover,"
Or cards from people off on journeys,
Or formal statements from attorneys.

The post came in. He let it lie.
    (All this biographers agree on.)
Especially he did not reply
    To things that had R.S.V.P. on.
Sometimes for months he dropped no lines
To dear ones, or sent Valentines;

But, polishing a second act
    Or coaxing kings to license Freedom,
Let his epistles wait. In fact,
    They say he didn't even read'm.
The which, some mornings, seems to me
A glorious blow for Liberty.

Brave Celt! Although one must deplore
    His manners, and with reason ample,
How bright from duty's other shore,
    This moment, seems his bold example!
And would I owned in equal balance
His courage (and, of course, his talents),

Who, using up his mail to start
    An autumn fire or chink a crevice,
Cried, "Letters longer are than art,
    But *vita* is extremely *brevis!*"
Then, choosing what was worth the candle,
Sat down and wrote *The School for Scandal.*

Portrait of Girl with Comic Book

Thirteen's no age at all. Thirteen is nothing.
It is not wit, or powder on the face,
Or Wednesday matinées, or misses' clothing,
Or intellect, or grace.
Twelve has its tribal customs. But thirteen
Is neither boys in battered cars nor dolls,
Not *Sara Crewe,* or movie magazine,
Or pennants on the walls.

Thirteen keeps diaries and tropical fish
(A month, at most); scorns jumpropes in the spring;
Could not, would fortune grant it, name its wish;
Wants nothing, everything;
Has secrets from itself, friends it despises;
Admits none to the terrors that it feels;
Owns half a hundred masks but no disguises;
And walks upon its heels.

Thirteen's anomalous—not that, not this:
Not folded bud, or wave that laps a shore,
Or moth proverbial from the chrysalis.
Is the one age defeats the metaphor.
Is not a town, like childhood, strongly walled
But easily surrounded; is no city.
Nor, quitted once, can it be quite recalled—
Not even with pity.

In Praise of Diversity

Phi Beta Kappa Poem, Columbia University, 1953

Since this ingenious earth began
　　To shape itself from fire and rubble;
Since God invented man, and man
　　At once fell to, inventing trouble,
One virtue, one subversive grace
Has chiefly vexed the human race.

One whimsical beatitude,
　　Concocted for his gain and glory,
Has man most stoutly misconstrued
　　Of all the primal category—
Counting no blessing, but a flaw,
That Difference is the mortal law.

Adam, perhaps, while toiling late,
　　With life a book still strange to read in,
Saw his new world, how variegate,
　　And mourned, "It was not so in Eden,"
Confusing thus from the beginning
Unlikeness with original sinning.

And still the sons of Adam's clay
    Labor in person or by proxy
At altering to a common way
    The planet's holy heterodoxy.
Till now, so dogged is the breed,
Almost it seems that they succeed.

One shrill, monotonous, level note
    The human orchestra's reduced to.
Man casts his ballot, turns his coat,
    Gets born, gets buried as he used to,
Makes war, makes love—but with a kind
Of masked and universal mind.

His good has no nuances. He
    Doubts or believes with total passion.
Heretics choose for heresy
    Whatever's the prevailing fashion.
Those wearing Tolerance for a label
Call other views intolerable.

"For or Against" 's the only rule.
    Damned are the unconvinced, the floaters.
Now all must go to public school,
    March with the League of Women Voters,
Or else for safety get allied
With a unanimous Other Side.

There's white, there's black; no tint between.
  Truth is a plane that was a prism.
All's Blanshard that's not Bishop Sheen.
  All's treason that's not patriotism.
Faith, charity, hope—now all must fit
One pattern or its opposite.

Or so it seems. Yet who would dare
  Deny that nature planned it other,
When every freckled thrush can wear
  A dapple various from his brother,
When each pale snowflake in the storm
Is false to some imagined norm?

Recalling then what surely was
  The earliest bounty of Creation:
That not a blade among the grass
  But flaunts its difference with elation,
Let us devoutly take no blame
If similar does not mean the same.

And grateful for the wit to see
  Prospects through doors we cannot enter,
Ah! let us praise Diversity
  Which holds the world upon its center.
Praise *con amor'* or *furioso*
The large, the little, and the soso.

Rejoice that under cloud and star
    The planet's more than Maine or Texas.
Bless the delightful fact there are
    Twelve months, nine muses, and two sexes;
And infinite in earth's dominions
Arts, climates, wonders, and opinions.

Praise ice and ember, sand and rock,
    Tiger and dove and ends and sources;
Space travelers, and who only walk
    Like mailmen round familiar courses;
Praise vintage grapes and tavern Grappas,
And bankers and Phi Beta Kappas;

Each in its moment justified,
    Praise knowledge, theory, second guesses;
That which must wither or abide;
    Prim men, and men like wildernesses;
And men of peace and men of mayhem
And pipers and the ones who pay 'em.

Praise the disheveled, praise the sleek;
    Austerity and hearts-and-flowers;
People who turn the other cheek
    And extroverts who take cold showers;
Saints we can name a holy day for
And infidels the saints can pray for.

Praise youth for pulling things apart,
   Toppling the idols, breaking leases;
Then from the upset apple-cart
   Praise oldsters picking up the pieces.
Praise wisdom, hard to be a friend to,
And folly one can condescend to.

Praise what conforms and what is odd,
   Remembering, if the weather worsens
Along the way, that even God
   Is said to be three separate Persons.
Then upright or upon the knee,
Praise Him that by His courtesy,
For all our prejudice and pains,
Diverse His Creature still remains.

Ballade of Lost Objects

Where are the ribbons I tie my hair with?
    Where is my lipstick? Where are my hose—
The sheer ones hoarded these weeks to wear with
    Frocks the closets do not disclose?
Perfumes, petticoats, sports chapeaux,
    The blouse Parisian, the earring Spanish—
Everything suddenly ups and goes.
    And where in the world did the children vanish?

This is the house I used to share with
    Girls in pinafores, shier than does.
I can recall how they climbed my stair with
    Gales of giggles, on their tiptoes.
Last seen wearing both braids and bows
    (But looking rather Raggedy-Annish),
When they departed nobody knows—
    Where in the world did the children vanish?

Two tall strangers, now, I must bear with,
    Decked in my personal furbelows,
Raiding the larder, rending the air with
    Gossip and terrible radios.
Neither my friends nor quite my foes,
    Alien, beautiful, stern, and clannish,
Here they dwell, while the wonder grows:
    Where in the world did the children vanish?

Prince, I warn you, under the rose,
  Time is the thief you cannot banish.
These are my daughters, I suppose.
  But where in the world did the children vanish?

Love Letter to an Institution

Of all museums,
I've a pet museum,
And it's not the Morgan
Or the Met Museum,
Or the Frick Museum,
Which steals the heart,
Or a trick museum
Like the Modern Art.
I must confess
It's a queer museum,
A more or less
Done-by-ear museum,
But it suits my nature
As knife suits fork:
The Museum of the City of New York.

A bit like an auction,
A bit like a fair,
Everything is cozy that's collected there.
Everything is cheerful as a Currier & Ives:
Capes made for gentlemen,
Caps for their wives;
Lamps lit at dark
By Great-Grandmama;
Central Park
In a diorama

(Where boys are sledding
And their runners curl);
A brownstone wedding
With a flower girl;
Doll-house parlors with carpet on the floor;
Patriotic posters from the First World War;
A solitary spur
That belonged to Aaron Burr;
And a small-scale model
Of a ten-cent store.

There for the dawdler,
Yesterday is spread—
Toys that a toddler
Carried once to bed;
Hoopskirts, horsecars,
Flags aplenty;
Somebody's dance dress, circa '20;
Somebody's platter, somebody's urn;
Mr. and Mrs.
Isaac Stern—
All gaily jumbled
So it's automatic
To believe you've stumbled
On your great-aunt's attic.
Helter-skelter
But large as life,
A room by Belter
And a room by Phyfe;
A period spinet,
A period speller;

The rooms that soured Mr. Rockefeller;
Rooms you can stare at, rooms you can poke in,
And a tenderhearted lobby
You can even smoke in.

It's a fine museum,
Not a new museum,
But a neighborly
Sort of old-shoe museum,
Not a class museum
Where the pundits go
Or a mass museum
With a Sunday show,
Not vast and grand
Like the Natural History.
How it ever got planned
Is a minor mystery.
But it fits my fancy
Like applesauce and pork,
The Museum of the City of New York.

Song of High Cuisine

(Written upon reading in the *New York Times* that Bloomingdale's grocery department now offers stuffed larks from the region of Carcassonne as well as one thrush from the French Alps)

At Bloomingdale's,
At Bloomingdale's,
 Who would not wish to be—
Where hornèd are the Gallic snails,
 Where curls the anchovy!
For palate stales as winter fails
 And rainy spring comes on.
So they have birds at Bloomingdale's
 That flew in Carcassonne.

Yes, hark!
The lark
At heaven's gate,
 That lately sang so pure,
There trussed and truffled for the plate
 Invites the epicure.
And, sheltering from the Alpine wind
 In more than Alpine hush,
Arrives most elegantly tinned
 A solitary thrush.

Ah, few the sales
 At Bloomingdale's,
   Amid imported straw,
Of tongues of foreign nightingales
   Or pearls in Malaga.
But they have many a merry thing.
   So who'll go there to buy
The little larks with parsleyed wing
That speak so eloquent of spring,
The single thrush that does not sing?

   Well, gentlemen, not I.

Of the small gifts of heaven,
It seems to me a more than equal share
At birth was given
To girls with curly hair.
Oh, better than being born with a silver ladle,
Or even with a caul on,
Is wearing ringlets sweetly from the cradle!
Slaves to no beauty salon,
Ladies whose locks grow prettier when moister
Can call the world their oyster.

Ladies with curly hair
Have time to spare.
Beneath a windy drier
They need not thumb through *Photoplay* each week.
They can look higher.
Efficient, tidy, and forever chic,
They own free hours to cook or study Greek,
Run for the Senate, answer notes, break par,
Write poems, chair the local D.A.R.,
Paint,
Or practice for a saint.

Ladies with curls are kind, being confident.
In smiles their lives are spent,
Primrosed their path.
Rising, like Venus, crinkly from the bath,
They keep appointments, punctual to the dot,
And do good works a lot.
In crises they are cool. 'Mid floods or wrecks,
Examples to their sex,
Steadfast they stand,
Calm in the knowledge not a hapless strand
Of hair is straggling down the backs of their necks.

However brief their lashes, plump their ankles,
The matter never rankles.
They marry well, are favorites with their kin.
Untyrannized by net and bobby pin,
They seldom cry "Alas!"
Or wring their hands or need divorce attorneys.
They are the girls boys choose at dancing class,
And they are beautiful on motor journeys.

Ah, pity her, however rose-and-white,
Who goes to bed at night
In clamps and clips!
Hers is no face to lure a thousand ships.
Had she been born unwavy,
Not Helen herself could ever have launched a navy.

Eros in the Kitchen

Our cook is in love. Love hangs on the house like a mist.
It embraces us all.
The spoons go uncounted. Confused is the grocery list,
But light each footfall.
Astonished, we notice how lyric the dishwasher sings.
(Did it always sing thus?)
And the mop has a lilt. And the telephone ceaselessly rings,
Although seldom for us.
Here nothing seems quite the same as it did before.
Something ineffably hovers
Over the household. All of us plunge or soar
With the mood of the lovers.
We dine to distraction on delicate viands today
Who, likely, tomorrow
Must scrabble with timorous forks at a fallen soufflé
More sodden than sorrow.
And salad's served up with dessert and the napkin's forgot,
The butter's unformed by the mold,
And the bouillon's barbarically cold,
Or the aspic comes hot.
And the message for Mister or Madam's a fortnight untold.

But who's such a churl as to care
With amour like a mist on the air,
On the house like a bloom—
When so blithe is the broom,

And the voice of the kettle, the beat of the brush on the tile
Sound gayer than springtime peeper?
We smile at each other at breakfast. At dinner we smile.
There's a smile on the face of the sleeper.
Our years have grown younger. We sally to parties at night
In tall hat and long glove.
We remember what we had forgotten. The hallways are bright.
Our cook is in love.

Main Street is gay. Each lamppost glimmers,
    Crowned with a blue, electric star.
The gift tree by our fountain shimmers,
    Superbly tall, if angular
    (Donated by the Men's Bazaar).

With garlands proper to the times
    Our doors are wreathed, our lintels strewn.
From our two steeples sound the chimes,
    Incessant, through the afternoon,
    Only a little out of tune.

Breathless with boxes hard to handle,
    The grocery drivers come and go.
Madam the Chairman lights a candle
    To introduce our club's tableau.
    The hopeful children pray for snow.

They cluster, mittened, in the park
    To talk of morning, half affrighted,
And early comes the winter dark
    And early are our windows lighted
    To wheedle homeward the benighted.

The eggnog's lifted for libation,
    Silent at last the postman's ring,
But on the plaza near the station
    The carolers are caroling.

"O Little Town!" the carolers sing.

Saturday Storm

This flooded morning is no time to be
Abroad on any business of mankind.
The rain has lost its casual charity;
It falls and falls and falls and would not mind
Were all the world washed blind.

No creature out of doors goes weatherproof.
Birds cower in their nests. The beast that can
Has found himself a roof.
This hour's for man
To waken late in, putter by his fire,
Leaf through old books or tear old letters up,
Mend household things with bits of thrifty wire,
Refill his coffee cup,
And, thus enclosed in comfort like a shell,
Give thought to, wish them well
Who must this day
On customary errands take their way:

The glistening policemen in the street,
For instance, blowing their whistles through the welter
And stamping their wet feet;
And grocery boys flung in and out of shelter
But faithful to their loads;
And people changing tires beside the roads;
Doormen with colds and doctors in damp suits;

And milkmen on their routes,
Scuttling like squirrels; and men with cleated boots
Aloft on telephone poles in the rough gale;
But chiefly trudging men with sacks of mail
Slung over shoulder,
Who slog from door to door and cannot rest
Till they've delivered the last government folder,
The final scribbled postcard, misaddressed.

Oh, all at ease
Should say a prayer for these—
That they come, healthy, homeward before night,
Safer than beasts or birds,
To no dark welcome but an earned delight
Of pleasant words,
Known walls, accustomed love, fires burning steady,
And a good dinner ready.

🦜 Sunday Psalm

This is the day which the Lord hath made,
Shining like Eden absolved of sin,
Three parts glitter to one part shade:
Let us be glad and rejoice therein.

Everything's scoured brighter than metal.
Everything sparkles as pure as glass—
The leaf on the poplar, the zinnia's petal,
The wing of the bird, and the blade of the grass.

All, all is luster. The glossy harbor
Dazzles the gulls that, gleaming, fly.
Glimmers the wasp on the grape in the arbor.
Glisten the clouds in the polished sky.

Tonight—tomorrow—the leaf will fade,
The waters tarnish, the dark begin.
But *this is the day which the Lord hath made:*
Let us be glad and rejoice therein.

The Doll House

After the children left it, after it stood
For a while in the attic,
Along with the badminton set, and the skis too good
To be given away, and the Peerless Automatic
Popcorn Machine that used to fly into rages,
And the Dr. Dolittle books, and the hamsters' cages,
She brought it down once more
To a bedroom, empty now, on the second floor
And put the furniture in.

> There was nothing much
That couldn't be used again with a bit of repair.
It was all there,
Perfect and little and inviolate.
So, with the delicate touch
A jeweler learns, she mended the rocking chair,
Meticulously laundered
The gossamer parlor curtains, dusted the grate,
Glued the glazed turkey to the flowered plate,
And polished the Lilliput writing desk.

> She squandered
One bold October day and half the night
Binding the carpets round with a ribbon border;
Till, to her grave delight
(With the kettle upon the stove, the mirror's face
Scoured, the formal sofa set in its place),
She saw the dwelling decorous and in order.

It was a good house. It had been artfully built
By an idle carpenter once, when the times were duller.
The windows opened and closed. The knocker was gilt.
And every room was painted a suitable color
Or papered to scale
For the sake of the miniature Adam and Chippendale.
And there were proper hallways,
Closets, lights, and a staircase. (What had always
Pleased her most
Was the tiny, exact, mahogany newel post.)
And always, too, wryly she thought to herself,
Absently pinning
A drapery's pleat, smoothing a cupboard shelf—
Always, from the beginning,
This outcome had been clear. Ah! She had known
Since the first clapboard was fitted, first rafter hung
(Yet not till now had known that she had known),
This was no daughters' fortune but her own—
Something cautiously lent to the careless young
To dazzle their cronies with for a handful of years
Till the season came
When their toys diminished to programs and souvenirs,
To tousled orchids, diaries well in arrears,
Anonymous snapshots stuck round a mirror frame,
Or letters locked away.

                                    Now seed of the past
Had fearfully flowered. Wholly her gift at last,
Here was her private estate, a peculiar treasure
Cut to her fancy's measure.
Now there was none to trespass, no one to mock
The extravagance of her sewing or her spending

(The tablecloth stitched out of lace, the grandfather's clock,
Stately upon the landing,
With its hands eternally pointing to ten past five).

Now all would thrive.

Over this house, most tranquil and complete,
Where no storm ever beat,
Whose innocent stair
No messenger ever climbed on quickened feet
With tidings either of rapture or of despair,
She was sole mistress. Through the panes she was able
To peer at her world reduced to the size of dream
But pure and unaltering.
                              There stood the dinner table,
Invincibly agleam
With the undisheveled candles, the flowers that bloomed
Forever and forever,
The wine that never
Spilled on the cloth or sickened or was consumed.

The *Times* lay at the doorsill, but it told
Daily the same unstirring report. The fire
Painted upon the hearth would not turn cold,
Or the constant hour change, or the heart tire
Of what it must pursue,
Or the guest depart, or anything here be old.

"Nor ever," she whispered, "bid the spring adieu."

And caught into this web of quietnesses
Where there was neither After nor Before,
She reached her hand to stroke the unwithering grasses
Beside the small and incorruptible door.

Midcentury Love Letter

Stay near me. Speak my name. Oh, do not wander
By a thought's span, heart's impulse, from the light
We kindle here. You are my sole defender
(As I am yours) in this precipitous night,
Which over earth, till common landmarks alter,
Is falling, without stars, and bitter cold.
We two have but our burning selves for shelter.
Huddle against me. Give me your hand to hold.

So might two climbers lost in mountain weather
On a high slope and taken by the storm,
Desperate in the darkness, cling together
Under one cloak and breathe each other warm.
Stay near me. Spirit, perishable as bone,
In no such winter can survive alone.

A GALLERY OF ELDERS

The Old Feminist

Snugly upon the equal heights
    Enthroned at last where she belongs,
She takes no pleasure in her Rights
    Who so enjoyed her Wrongs.

The Old Politician

Toward caution all his lifetime bent,
    Straddler and compromiser, he
Becomes a Public Monument
    Through sheer longevity.

The Old Reformer

Few friends he kept that pleased his mind.
His marriage failed when it began,
Who worked unceasing for mankind
But loathed his fellow man.

The Old Actor

Too lined for Hamlet, on the whole;
For tragic Lear, too coarsely built,
Himself becomes his favorite role,
Played daily to the hilt.

The Old Prelate

God's House such decades has been his
    To tend, through fortune or disaster,
He half forgets now which he is—
    Custodian or Master.

The Old Philanthropist

His millions make museums bright;
    Harvard anticipates his will;
While his young typist weeps at night
    Over a druggist's bill.

The Old Beauty

Coquettes with doctors; hoards her breath
    For blandishments; fluffs out her hair;
And keeps her stubborn suitor, Death,
    Moping upon the stair.

The Old Radical

The burning cause that lit his days
    When he was younger came to harm.
Now Hate's impoverished charcoal blaze
    Is all that keeps him warm.

The Temptations of Saint Anthony

Off in the wilderness bare and level,
Anthony wrestled with the Devil.
Once he'd beaten the Devil down,
Anthony'd turn his eyes toward town
And leave his hermitage now and then
To come to grips with the souls of men.

Afterward, all the tales agree,
Wrestling the Devil seemed to be
Quite a relief to Anthony.

Lesson for Beginners

Martin of Tours,
When he earned his shilling
Trooping the flags
Of the Roman Guard,
Came on a poor,
Aching and chilling
Beggar in rags
By the barracks yard.

Blind to his lack,
The Guard went riding.
But Martin a moment
Paused and drew
The coat from his back,
His sword from hiding,
And sabered his raiment
Into two.

Now some who muse
On the allegory
Affect to find
It a pious joke;
To the beggar what use,
For Martin what glory,
In deed half-kind
And part of a cloak?

Still, it has charm
And a point worth seizing.
For all who move
In the mortal sun
Know halfway warm
Is better than freezing,
As half a love
Is better than none.

🦋 *The Giveaway*

Saint Bridget was
A problem child.
Although a lass
Demure and mild,
And one who strove
To please her dad,
Saint Bridget drove
The family mad.
For here's the fault in Bridget lay:
She *would* give everything away.

To any soul
Whose luck was out
She'd give her bowl
Of stirabout;
She'd give her shawl,
Divide her purse
With one or all.
And what was worse,
When she ran out of things to give
She'd borrow from a relative.

Her father's gold,
Her grandsire's dinner,
She'd hand to cold
And hungry sinner;

Give wine, give meat,
No matter whose;
Take from her feet
The very shoes,
And when her shoes had gone to others,
Fetch forth her sister's and her mother's.

She could not quit.
She had to share;
Gave bit by bit
The silverware,
The barnyard geese,
The parlor rug,
Her little niece-
'S christening mug,
Even her bed to those in want,
And then the mattress of her aunt.

An easy touch
For poor and lowly,
She gave so much
And grew so holy
That when she died
Of years and fame,
The countryside
Put on her name,
And still the Isles of Erin fidget
With generous girls named Bride or Bridget.

2

Well, one must love her.
Nonetheless,
In thinking of her
Givingness,
There's no denial
She must have been
A sort of trial
To her kin.
The moral, too, seems rather quaint.
Who had the patience of a saint,
From evidence presented here?
Saint Bridget? Or her near and dear?

When Philip Neri walked abroad
Beside the Tiber, praising God,
They say he was attended home
By half the younger set of Rome.

Knight, novice, scholar, boisterous boy,
They followed after him with joy,
To nurse his poor and break his bread
And hear the funny things he said.

For Philip Neri (by his birth
A Florentine) believed in mirth,
Holding that virtue took no harm
Which went with laughter arm-in-arm.

Two books he read with most affection—
The Gospels and a joke collection;
And sang hosannas set to fiddles
And fed the sick on soup and riddles.

So when the grave rebuke the merry,
Let them remember Philip Neri
(Fifteen-fifteen to ninety-five),
Who was the merriest man alive,
Then, dying at eighty or a bit,
Became a saint by Holy Wit.

Conversation in Avila

Teresa was God's familiar. She often spoke
To Him informally,
As if together they shared some heavenly joke.
Once, watching stormily
Her heart's ambitions wither to odds and ends,
With all to start anew,
She cried, "If this is the way You treat Your friends,
No wonder You have so few!"

There is, however, no record standing by
Of God's reply.

On top of a pillar Simeon sat.
He wore no mantle,
He had no hat,
But bare as a bird
Sat night and day.
And hardly a word
Did Simeon say.

Under the sun of the desert sky
He sat on a pillar
Nine feet high.
When Fool and his brother
Came round to admire,
He raised it another
Nine feet high'r.

The seasons circled about his head.
He lived on water
And crusts of bread
(Or so one hears)
From pilgrims' store,
For thirty years
And a little more.

And why did Simeon sit like that,
Without a garment,
Without a hat,
In a holy rage
For the world to see?
It puzzles the age,
It puzzles me.
It puzzled many
A Desert Father.
And I think it puzzled the Good Lord, rather.

Gossiping in Siena's square,
    The housewife, Lapa, used to say,
"My Catherine has yellow hair
    Like the True Princess in the play.
    Sure as it's June that follows May,
Our Kate was born to be a belle.
    The girl's a clever one, and gay.
I plan for her to marry well."

Lapa had hopes; would not despair.
    "The young ones always fast and pray
A season," Lapa would declare.
    "This holy nonsense does not stay."
    Though all Siena thronged to pay
Homage to Catherine in her cell,
    Stubbornly Lapa bragged away,
"I plan for her to marry well."

They pressed from nations everywhere,
    Poet, prince, prelate, common clay,
To gape at genius. On the stair,
    Their feet were clamorous night and day.
    She saw the very Pope obey
The summons Catherine scarce could spell
    And muttered, "What's a slight delay?
I plan for her to marry well."

Still muttered as the world turned gray,
   "How pretty her hair was! Who could tell
That things would go so far astray?
   I planned for her to marry well."

Paterfamilias

Of all the saints who have won their charter—
Holy man, hero, hermit, martyr,
Mystic, missioner, sage, or wit—
Saint Thomas More is my favorite.
For he loved these bounties with might and main:
God and his house and his little wife, Jane,
And four fair children his heart throve on,
Margaret, Elizabeth, Cecily, and John.

That More was a good man everybody knows.
He sang good verses and he wrote good prose,
Enjoyed a good caper and liked a good meal
And made a good Master of the Privy Seal.
A friend to Erasmus, Lily's friend,
He lived a good life and he had a good end
And left good counsel for them to con,
Margaret, Elizabeth, Cecily, and John.

Some saints are alien, hard to love,
Wild as an eagle, strange as a dove,
Too near to heaven for the mind to scan.
But Thomas More was a family man,
A husband, a courtier, a doer and a hoper
(Admired of his son-in-law, Mr. Roper),
Who punned in Latin like a Cambridge don
With Margaret, Elizabeth, Cecily, and John.

It was less old Henry than Anne Boleyn
Haled him to the Tower and locked him in.
But even in the Tower he saw things brightly.
He spoke to his jailers most politely,
And while the sorrowers turned their backs
He rallied the headsman who held the ax,
Then blessed, with the blessing of Thomas More,
God and his garden and his children four.

And I fear they missed him when he was gone—
Margaret, Elizabeth, Cecily, and John.

Blind Francis, waiting to welcome Sister Death,
Worn though he was by ecstasies and fame,
Had heart for tune. With what remained of breath
He led his friars in canticles.

                    Then came
Brother Elias, scowling, to his side,
Small-souled Elias, crying by book and candle,
This was outrageous! Had the monks no pride?
Music at deathbeds! Ah, the shame, the scandal!

Elias gave him sermons and advice
Instead of song; which simply proves once more
What things are sure this side of paradise:
Death, taxes, and the counsel of the bore.
Though we outwit the tithe, make death our friend,
Bores we have with us even to the end.

God's angry man, His crotchety scholar,
Was Saint Jerome,
The great name-caller,
Who cared not a dime
For the laws of libel
And in his spare time
Translated the Bible.
Quick to disparage
All joys but learning,
Jerome thought marriage
Better than burning;
But didn't like woman's
Painted cheeks;
Didn't like Romans,
Didn't like Greeks,
Hated Pagans
For their Pagan ways,
Yet doted on Cicero all his days.

A born reformer, cross and gifted,
He scolded mankind
Sterner than Swift did;
Worked to save
The world from the heathen;
Fled to a cave
For peace to breathe in,

Promptly *where*with
For miles around
He filled the air with
Fury and sound.
In a mighty prose
For almighty ends,
He thrust at his foes,
Quarreled with his friends,
And served his Master,
Though with complaint.
He wasn't a plaster sort of saint.

But he swelled men's minds
With a Christian leaven.
It takes all kinds
To make a Heaven.

A LITTLE BLAME

When blithe to argument I come,
  Though armed with facts, and merry,
May Providence protect me from
  The fool as adversary,
Whose mind to him a kingdom is
  Where reason lacks dominion,
Who calls conviction prejudice
  And prejudice opinion.

Yes, when with dolts I disagree,
  Both *sic* and also *semper,*
May my good angels succor me
  And help me hold my temper.
But strength from what celestial store
  Shall keep my head from bending
When I behold whom I abhor—
The snob, the bigot, and the bore—
Wielding their witless cudgels for
  The cause that I'm defending?

The Day After Sunday

Always on Monday, God's in the morning papers,
    His Name is a headline, His Works are rumored abroad.
Having been praised by men who are movers and shapers,
    From prominent Sunday pulpits, newsworthy is God.

On page 27, just opposite Fashion Trends,
    One reads at a glance how He scolded the Baptists a little,
Was firm with the Catholics, practical with the Friends,
    To Unitarians pleasantly noncommittal.

In print are His numerous aspects, too: God smiling,
    God vexed, God thunderous, God whose mansions are pearl,
Political God, God frugal, God reconciling
    Himself with science, God guiding the Camp Fire Girl.

Always on Monday morning the press reports
    God as revealed to His vicars in various guises—
Benevolent, stormy, patient, or out of sorts.
    God knows which God is the God God recognizes.

Publisher's Party

At tea in cocktail weather,
  The lady authors gather.
Their hats are made of feather.
  They talk of Willa Cather.

They talk of Proust and Cather,
  And how we drift, and whither.
Where wends the lady author,
  Martinis do not wither.

Their cocktails do not wither
  Nor does a silence hover.
That critic who comes hither
  Is periled like a lover;

Is set on like a lover.
  Alert and full of power,
They flush him from his cover,
  No matter where he cower.

And Honor Guest must cower
  When they, descending rather
Like bees upon a flower,
  Demand his views on Cather—

On Wharton, James, or Cather,
  Or Eliot or Luther,
Or Joyce or Cotton Mather,
  Or even Walter Reuther.

In fact, the tracts of Reuther
  They will dispute together
For hours, gladly, soother
  Than fall on silent weather.

From teas in any weather
Where lady authors gather,
Whose hats are largely feather,
Whose cocktails do not wither,
Who quote from Proust and Cather
(With penitence toward neither),
Away in haste I slither,
Feeling I need a breather.

⟡ Lines Scribbled on a Program

(AND DISCOVERED BY A WAITER SWEEPING UP AFTER
A LITERARY DINNER)

Whenever public speakers rise
    To dazzle hearers and beholders,
A film comes over both my eyes.
    Inevitably, toward my shoulders
I feel my head begin to sink.
It is an allergy, I think.

No matter what the time or place,
    No matter how adroit the speaker
Or rich the tone or famed the face,
    I feel my life force ebbing weaker.
Even the chairman, lauding him,
Can make the room about me swim.

The room swims. And my palms are wet.
    Languor and lassitude undo me.
I fumble with a cigarette
    For ashtrays never handy to me,
Lift chin, grit teeth, shift in my chair,
But nothing helps—not even prayer.

From all who Talk, I dream away—
　　From statesmen heavy with their travels,
From presidents of P.T.A.
　　Exchanging honorary gavels;
From prelate, pedant, wit, and clown,
Club treasurer, John Mason Brown;

From lecturers on the ductless gland,
　　Ex-Communists, ex-dukes, exhorters,
Poets with poems done by hand,
　　Political ladies, lady reporters,
Professors armed with bell and book,
Mimes, magnates, mayors, Alistair Cooke.

The hot, the fluent, and the wise,
　　The dull, the quick-upon-the-trigger—
Alike, alike they close my eyes.
　　Alike they rob me of my vigor.
For me Demosthenes, with pain,
Had mouthed his Attic stones in vain.

The aforementioned being clear
　　Concerning speech, concerning speaker,
Alas, what am I doing here,
　　Facing my empty plate and beaker,
And watching with a wild unrest
The rising of the evening's Guest?
Ah, was it mine, this monstrous choice?
Whose accents these? And whose the voice
That wakes in me a pang well known?

Good God, it is my own, my own!

Sticks and stones are hard on bones.
Aimed with angry art,
Words can sting like anything.
But silence breaks the heart.

How vast, how clean
   The ageless ocean!
Whether serene
   Or in commotion,
Haunted by gull
   Or dolphin set,
How beautiful,
   How wild and wet!

Though rich and rare
   Its fauna and flora,
No evening's there
   And no aurora;
Instead, I think,
   A great supply
Of pearls and ink-
   Y octopi.

From pole to pole
   What whales take cover in,
The moon its sole
   Capricious sovereign,
Speaking in thunders
   Through its sleep,
Ah, rife with wonders
   Is the deep!

The waters tell it,
The billows shout it.
And I'm fed to the teeth with books about it.

Do they need any rain
In Portland, Maine?
   Does Texas pray for torrents,
The water supply
Run dry, run dry,
   From the ancient wells of Florence?
Is the vintage grape
In perilous shape
   On the slopes of Burgundy?
Let none despair
At the arid air—
   They've only to send for me.
Invite me to stay for a holiday
   And the rain will follow me.

Rain is my lover, my apple strudel.
It haunts my heels like a pedigreed poodle.
Beyond the seas or across the nation,
It follows me faithful on every vacation.

Others back from Bermuda wander
Burning pink as an oleander.
But sun turns off like a Macy gadget
The minute I set a foot in Paget.

It rains when I go to a Brookline wedding.
Friday to Monday it rains in Redding.
All that I've seen of a bay called Oyster
Is part of the ocean getting moister.

The tops of umbrellas was all I saw,
The time I attended the Mardi Gras.
And it hadn't rained for a year in Tucson
Till I was the guest the clouds let loose on.

Wherever I travel, wherever I hie,
Tumult begins in the cumuli,
The mold creeps over the pillow's feather,
And flaps of envelopes stick together.

I never land
With my bags in hand
   But floods inspire the greenery.
I bring fresh showers
For the thirsting flowers
   But I don't see much of the scenery.
The desert's a rose where I am, God knows,
   But I don't see much of the scenery.

So Noah was lucky, I guess, at that,
I wasn't weekending on Ararat.

Man with Pruning Shears

This gentleman loves all that grows—
    Bud, shoot, or bough that blossoms dapple.
He plants the rose and feeds the rose
    And guards the springtime apple;

Has a green thumb; is quick to praise
    The frailest petal in his borders;
Can heal (and with a myriad sprays)
    The peony's disorders.

So what has overtaken him,
    What frenzy set his wits to wander
That he should ravage limb by limb
    The wholesome lilac yonder?

That he should lay the privet low
    And do the vines such deadly treason
That scarce a twig, I think, will show
    Its leaf again this season?

A milder chap was never planned,
    Or one who dug with more decorum.
But now the weapon's in his hand,
    And branches thick before'm.

The selfsame madness takes his mind
    That took his mind when he was little
And owned a knife and could not find
    Sufficient sticks to whittle.

I wish I owned a Dior dress
    Made to my order out of satin.
I wish I weighed a little less
    And could read Latin,
Had perfect pitch or matching pearls,
    A better head for street directions,
And seven daughters, all with curls
    And fair complexions.
I wish I'd tan instead of burn.
    But most, on all the stars that glisten,
I wish at parties I could learn
    To sit and listen.

I wish I didn't talk so much at parties.
It isn't that I want to hear
My voice assaulting every ear,
Uprising loud and firm and clear
    Above the cocktail clatter.
It's simply, once a doorbell's rung,
(I've been like this since I was young)
Some madness overtakes my tongue
    And I begin to chatter.

Buffet, ball, banquet, quilting bee,
  Wherever conversation's flowing,
Why must I feel it falls on me
  To keep things going?
Though ladies cleverer than I
  Can loll in silence, soft and idle,
Whatever topic gallops by,
  I seize its bridle,
Hold forth on art, dissect the stage,
  Or babble like a kindergart'ner
Of politics till I enrage
  My dinner partner.

I wish I didn't talk so much at parties.
When hotly boil the arguments,
Ah! would I had the common sense
To sit demurely on a fence
  And let who will be vocal,
Instead of plunging in the fray
With my opinions on display
Till all the gentlemen edge away
  To catch an early local.

Oh! there is many a likely boon
  That fate might flip me from her griddle.
I wish that I could sleep till noon
  And play the fiddle,
Or dance a *tour jeté* so light
  It would not shake a single straw down.
But when I ponder how last night
  I laid the law down,

More than to have the Midas touch
   Or critics' praise, however hearty,
I wish I didn't talk so much,
I wish I didn't talk *so much,*
I wish *I didn't talk so much*
   When I am at a party.

Homework for Annabelle

$A = bh$ over 2.
   3.14 is π.
But I'd forgotten, if I ever knew,
   What R's divided by.
Though I knew once, I'd forgotten clean
What a girl must study to reach fifteen—
How V is Volume and M's for Mass,
And the hearts of the young are brittle as glass.

I had forgotten, and half with pride,
   Fifteen's no field of clover.
So here I sit at Annabelle's side,
   Learning my lessons over.
For help is something you have to give
When daughters are faced with the Ablative
Or first encounter in any school
Immutable gender's mortal rule.

Day after day for a weary spell,
   When the dusk has pitched its tents,
I sit with a book and Annabelle
   At the hour of confidence
And rummage for lore I had long consigned
To cobwebby attics of my mind,
Like: For the Radius, write down R,
The Volga's a river, Vega's a star,

Brazil's in the Tropic of Capricorn,
And heart is a burden that has to be borne.

Oh, high is the price of parenthood,
    And daughters may cost you double.
You dare not forget, as you thought you could,
    That youth is a plague and trouble.
N times 7 is $7n$—
Here I go learning it all again:
The climates of continents tend to vary,
The verb "to love" 's not auxiliary,
Tomorrow will come and today will pass,
But the hearts of the young are brittle as glass.

A Word to Hostesses

Celebrities are lonely when
They congregate with lesser men.
Among less lambent men they sit,
Bereft of style, deprived of wit,
A little chilly to the touch,
And do not sparkle very much.

Wrenched from their coteries, they lack
Mirrors to send their image back,
And find it, therefore, hard to muster
Glint for a purely private luster.
(One sees a hunger in their eyes
For splendor they can recognize.)

But seat them next a Name, and lo!
How they most instantly will glow,
Will light the sky or heat the room
With gossip's incandescent bloom,
As if, like twigs, they only burst
In flame when rubbed together first.

Hostesses, then, when you are able
To lure Celebrity to table,
It is discreet to bear in mind
He needs the comfort of his kind.
Fetch other Names. Fetch three or four.

A dozen's better, or a score.
And half a hundred might be fitter.

But even one will make him glitter.

The Forgotten Woman

Who are the friends of Dr. Gallup? Who,
Ah, who are they
Incessantly he puts inquiries to—
The ones who say
Their public yea or nay
On every matter controversy flares in?

Who fills those questionnaires in?

Where lurk the people Mr. Roper's minions
Implore for their opinions?
What straws define the wind, however it blows?
God knows.
All I can vouch for is the fact I see:
Nobody quizzes *me*.

Day after day across this mighty land,
While thunderous presses roll,
Young men with hats and briefcases in hand
(Or so I understand)
Wander from poll to poll,
Asking odd men in some peculiar street
Which candidate is theirs, which breakfast food
They least dislike to eat,
Which heresy offends their current mood.

But, left or right though thick the issues fall,
Nobody asks me anything at all.

Although I hold opinions firm and ample,
Unmatched as clues,
Nobody begs me will I be his Sample.
None wants my views—
Not even Fotographers from the *Daily News.*

Never do wheedling voices at my door
Ask how I stand on Nembutal for naps,
Or Christian soldiers marching off to war,
Or love, or coonskin caps,
Which virtue I prefer, which cigarette.
I never get
Called to the phone by females I'm no kin to
To say which TV program I'm tuned in to.

The counters and the checkers pass me by.
Ignored am I
Alike by those who augur, for a stipend,
Just how the votes have ripened
And by distinguished *Time*men gathering data
On everybody else's Alma Mata.

Still, hope's eternal. Here I stand and wait,
All needles-y and pins-y,
Thinking perhaps yon stranger at my gate
May come from Dr. Kinsey;
Might be, at worst, a messenger, delayed,
Seeking my choices for the Hit Parade.

But no one knocks to ask me, even now,
Am I detergent-minded or a soaper.
Where art thou, Gallup? Hooper, where art thou?
Where's Elmo Roper?
The breeze is freshening, the breeze is raw,
And here's your willing straw.
Before the unpolled generations trample me,
Won't *some*one sample me?

Mrs. Sweeney Among the Allegories

(Multi-Level Verses Composed in a New Haven Railroad Car Immediately after Having Spent an Afternoon with the *Collected Poems of T. S. Eliot* and an Evening at *The Confidential Clerk*)

1.

In the beginning was the word
    And, for an act, I understood.
Colby was Lord Mulhammer's son.
    Burnished Lucasta longed for food.

Gnomic, the jests of Ina Claire
    Scampered on super-cadenced feet.
Eggerson spoke of Brussels Sprouts.
    Entered, at left, the Paraclete.

Defunctive message under B.
    Passed comprehension after while,
Nearly; even I could see
    Discussion animate the aisle.

Transfigured, the illicit clerk
    Refused a post designed for him.
Play beneath play beneath a play
    Then burnt, just visible but dim.

2.

"This music crept by me upon the water,"
Along Times Square, cutting through Shubert Alley.
O! Poet's Poet, for a bit I heard,
Upon a little stool in the Algonquin,
The murmur of your transcendental meaning,
With all the fiddles of the mind beginning
To scratch it out. But then,
A single waiter with insomnia cried,
"Madam, your double bourbon," and it died.

3.

On the stage the actors come and go.
Whose heir is which they do not know.

4.

Between the Idea
 And the Interpretation,
Between the epigram
 And the guffaw,
              Falls the Symbol.

Between the Intermission
And the Finale,
Between the horns
And the dilemma,
                    Falls the Symbol.

Between the First Level
And the Third Level,
Between the dark
And the daylight,
Between Grand Central Terminal
And Larchmont, New York,
                    Falls the Symbol.

            Here, then, is the story:

5.

T. Eliot, the Anglican, who feared God,
    Removing his bowler, furling his umbrella,
Set down, in riddles, dogma for the crowd.
    Now he's in Africa with another fella,
Leaving behind no confidential Glossary.
I hope he's not run over by Rhinosauri.

6.

For
This is the way his farce ends,
This is the way his farce ends,
This is the way his farce ends,
Not with a mot but a moral.

MIXED BOUQUET

ALMOST ANY EVENING

On all the channels,
Nothing but panels!

PICKWICK TIME

Readings by Mr. Laughton
I cannot dote as I ought on.
Though the prose is doubtless
Deathless,
Could he not speak out less
Breathless?

MAMA

The humor of family sagas is far from Shavian—
Including the Scandinavian.

THE NEWS

Now that the crisp or thunderous word
Has been made flesh upon the screen,
The day's events a little blurred
Come to my ear. Ah, could it mean
Newscasters should be only heard,
Not seen?

REFLECTIONS DENTAL

How pure, how beautiful, how fine
Do teeth on television shine!
No flutist flutes, no dancer twirls,
But comes equipped with matching pearls.
Gleeful announcers all are born
With sets like rows of hybrid corn.
Clowns, critics, clergy, commentators,
Ventriloquists and roller skaters,
M.C.s who beat their palms together,
The girl who diagrams the weather,
The crooner crooning for his supper—
All flash white treasures, lower and upper.
With miles of smiles the airwaves teem,
And each an orthodontist's dream.

'Twould please my eye as gold a miser's—
One charmer with uncapped incisors.

DEFINITION OF AN AFTERNOON PROGRAM

A lady who shows you how to embellish
Saturday's roast with Monday's relish.

INSULT IS THE SOUL OF WIT

Groucho Marx is a man I'm fond of.
A gray-haired jest he can make a blonde of.
But I'd rather be a derelict, sleeping in parks,
Than a guest on the program of Groucho Marx.

ON THE PREVALENCE OF MURDER

Did I hear you say
Crime doesn't *pay?*

EIGHT-MILLION-DOLLAR BABY

The paeans rose and the anthems rang,
The Stars in their courses danced with joy,
Oh, even the *Herald Tribune* sang,
When Lucille Ball had a baby boy.
Now I shudder to think how unto infinity
Will roll the story of the Arnaz trinity.

🐚 *Love Letter to a Factory*

(Composed upon reading in the *New York Times* that each employee o
General Brass & Machine Works, Inc., will receive a day off with pay o
his birthday)

Hoist high the glass!
   Ah! Let us drink
To General Brass
   And Machine Works, Inc.,
Where every hand
Who earns his pay
Can sleep till noon on his natal day.

From tropic blaze
   To arctic bound'ry,
Who will not praise
   This noble foundry,
Which crowns its workers
Of either sex
Each a Regina or a Rex?

For what's the best
   Of benefits worth
Compared to a rest
   On the day of one's birth?
What is overtime?
What's a bonus?
Here is a gift without an onus—

The only holiday ever designed
To be enjoyed with a peaceful mind.

Humanity strains
    Its Christmas powers,
Assembling trains
    In the little hours.
The Fourth's unsafe
For a car to get out.
Memorial Day, it's always wet out.
Labor Day's hot, the New Year's infirm,
Washington's feast invites the germ,
While the turkey hid in Thanksgiving's straw
Is having to dine with one's brothers-in-law.
But a man's a king
Who sits and rocks
While the rest of the world is punching clocks.

So shout it to Lewis,
    Cry it to Quill—
A job to do is
    Before them still.
Away with pensions!
    Let's all set sights
Toward big conventions
    On Birthday Rights.
Tell Hoosier, Alaskan,
    Cape Codder, Mohican:
What General Brass can
    Do, A.T.&T. can,
Detroit can, Milan can,

And Steel can and Silk can,
American Can can
And Carnation Milk can,

Till, idling legal,
His personal morn,
Every man's regal
And glad he was born.

June in the Suburbs

Not with a whimper but a roar
Of birth and bloom this month commences.
The wren's a gossip at her door.
Roses explode along the fences.

By day the chattering mowers cope
With grass decreed a final winner.
Darkness delays. The skipping rope
Twirls in the driveway after dinner.

Through lupine-lighted borders now
For winter bones Dalmatians forage.
Costly, the spray on apple bough.
The canvas chair comes out of storage;

And rose-red golfers dream of par,
And class-bound children loathe their labors,
While pilgrims, touring gardens, are
Cold to petunias of their neighbors.

Now from damp loafers nightly spills
The sand. Brides lodge their lists with Plummer.
And cooks devise on charcoal grills
The first burnt offerings of summer.

Daniel at Breakfast

His paper propped against the electric toaster
   (Nicely adjusted to his morning use),
Daniel at breakfast studies world disaster
   And sips his orange juice.

The words dismay him. Headlines shrilly chatter
   Of famine, storm, death, pestilence, decay.
Daniel is gloomy, reaching for the butter.
   He shudders at the way

War stalks the planet still, and men know hunger,
   Go shelterless, betrayed, may perish soon.
The coffee's weak again. In sudden anger
   Daniel throws down his spoon

And broods a moment on the kitchen faucet
   The plumber mended, but has mended ill;
Recalls tomorrow means a dental visit,
   Laments the grocery bill.

Then, having shifted from his human shoulder
   The universal woe, he drains his cup,
Rebukes the weather (surely turning colder),
   Crumples his napkin up
And, kissing his wife abruptly at the door,
Stamps fiercely off to catch the 8:04.

Launcelot with Bicycle

Her window looks upon the lane.
From it, anonymous and shy,
Twice daily she can see him plain,
Wheeling heroic by.
She droops her cheek against the pane
And gives a little sigh.

Above him maples at their bloom
Shake April pollen down like stars
While he goes whistling past her room
Toward unimagined wars,
A tennis visor for his plume,
Scornful of handlebars.

And, counting over in her mind
His favors, gleaned like windfall fruit
(A morning when he spoke her kind,
An afterschool salute,
A number that she helped him find,
Once, for his paper route),

Sadly she twists a stubby braid
And closer to the casement leans—
A wistful and a lily maid
In moccasins and jeans,
Despairing from the seventh grade
To match his lordly teens.

And so she grieves in Astolat
(Where other girls have grieved the same)
For being young and therefore not
Sufficient to his fame—
Who will by summer have forgot
Grief, April, and his name.

Season at the Shore

Oh, not by sun and not by cloud
And not by whippoorwill, crying loud,
And not by the pricking of my thumbs,
Do I know the way that the summer comes.
Yet here on this seagull-haunted strand,
Hers is an omen I understand—
Sand:

Sand on the beaches,
    Sand at the door,
Sand that screeches
    On the new-swept floor;
In the shower, sand for the foot to crunch on;
Sand in the sandwiches spread for luncheon;
Sand adhesive to son and sibling,
From wallet sifting, from pockets dribbling;
Sand by the beaker
    Nightly shed
From odious sneaker;
    Sand in bed;
Sahara always in my seaside shanty
Like the sand in the voice
Of J. Durante.

Winter is mittens, winter is gaiters
Steaming on various radiators.
Autumn is leaves that bog the broom.
Spring is mud in the living room
Or skates in places one scarcely planned.
But what is summer, her seal and hand?
Sand:

Sand in the closets,
    Sand on the stair,
Desert deposits
    In the parlor chair;
Sand in the halls like the halls of ocean;
Sand in the soap and the sun-tan lotion;
Stirred in the porridge, tossed in the greens,
Poured from the bottoms of rolled-up jeans;
    In the elmy street,
        On the lawny acre;
    Glued to the seat
        Of the Studebaker;
Wrapped in the folds of the *Wall Street Journal;*
Damp sand, dry sand,
Sand eternal.

When I shake my garments at the Lord's command,
What will I scatter in the Promised Land?
Sand.

In June, on Sturges Highway
(Seven miles north of Westport),
From a worn, familiar meadow,
   Five prosperous cows will stare.
There will be stylish lilies,
Haughty, along the fences,
And butterflies, white and yellow,
   Embracing in upper air.
But what's Connecticut June to me?
I'll feast no more on the strawberry
That grew in the garden of my friend, D——.

D——, a gentleman farmer,
In his spare time wrote novels.
But novels are getting written
   By thousands, every day.
It was a purer harvest
Than literature or letters
That beckoned me in the summer
   To the house on Sturges Way.
Ah, it was heaven itself to be
Given permission to wander free
In the strawberry beds of my friend, D——!

Maybe on other acres
(Though I cannot quite believe it)
Has a fruit as aromatic,
　　As fiercely crimson, hung.
But never, I think, did berry,
From curling leaves uncovered,
Fall with such mortal sweetness
　　So ravishing on the tongue,
As the plump, the succulent strawberry
That (stained with juices, on hand and knee)
I plucked in the garden of my friend, D——.

Drunker with sweets and sunlight
Than the butterflies above me,
Raiding ambrosial borders,
　　I would go up and down;
Until at the turn of evening,
Lugging my brimming baskets,
I would return, reluctant,
　　To the Birdseye-haunted town.
But weep for glory that used to be!
Gone are the berries that pleasured me,
　　And even goner is my friend, D——.

For love comes even to Westport.
A small and fair-haired lady
Looked on the gentleman farmer,
　　Melting his heart like snow.
And now from Sturges Highway
Are berry and man uprooted.

Now lonely along the fences,
    Only the lilies grow.
Yes, now a farmer no more is he—
Merely a novelist furiously
Finishing Chapter Twenty-three.

And never, never, on land or sea,
For breakfast, dinner, luncheon, tea,
I'll taste of the vanished strawberry
That starred the gardens of my friend, D———.

Small-Town Parade

Below the lawns and picket fences,
    Just past the firehouse, half a block,
Sharp at eleven-five commences
    This ardent and memorial walk
    (Announced, last night, for ten o'clock).

Solemn, beneath the elmy arches,
    Neighbor and next-door neighbor meet.
For half the village forward marches
    To the school band's uncertain beat,
    And half is lined along the street.

O the brave show! O twirling baton!
    O drummer stepping smartly out!
O mayor, perspiring, with no hat on!
    O nurses' aid! O martial rout
    Of Bluebird, Brownie, Eagle Scout!

And at the rear, aloof and splendid,
    Lugging the lanterns of their pride,
O the red firemen, well attended
    By boys on bicycles who ride
    With envious reverence at their side!

The morning smells of buds and grasses.
　　Birds twitter louder than the flute.
And wives, as the procession passes,
　　Wave plodding husbands wild salute
　　From porches handy to the route.

Flags snap. And children, vaguely greeted,
　　Wander into the ranks a while.
The band, bemused but undefeated,
　　Plays Sousa, pedagogic style,
　　Clean to the Square—a measured mile.

Until at last by streets grown stony,
　　To the gray monument they bring
The wreath which is less testimony
　　To Death than Life, continuing
　　Through this and every other spring.

The Angry Man

The other day I chanced to meet
An angry man upon the street—
A man of wrath, a man of war,
A man who truculently bore
Over his shoulder, like a lance,
A banner labeled "Tolerance."

And when I asked him why he strode
Thus scowling down the human road,
Scowling, he answered, "I am he
Who champions total liberty—
Intolerance being, ma'am, a state
No tolerant man can tolerate.

"When I meet rogues," he cried, "who choose
To cherish oppositional views,
Lady, like this, and in this manner,
I lay about me with my banner
Till they cry mercy, ma'am." His blows
Rained proudly on prospective foes.

Fearful, I turned and left him there
Still muttering, as he thrashed the air,
"Let the Intolerant beware!"

A Kind of Love Letter to New York

Love is a mischief,
Love is a brat.
Love is, admittedly, blind as a bat.
Aimless his arrows as bundles from the stork.
So I'm in love with
The City of New York.

Raging by its rivers, thrusting at the sky,
Here towers Gotham, and here gape I,
Viewing with idolatry more than lenience
The City of Infinite Inconvenience.

Here on its image, harsher than a chromo,
I dote as a teen-ager dotes on Como.
As a chorine pants for the rinse peroxide,
So I for its air made of carbon monoxide,

For the strap in the subway, for the empty hansom,
For the five-flight walk-up at a monarch's ransom,
For the weather omens that tell no truth
And the wait for the hotel telephone booth.

Yes, dear to my heart as to Midas his coffers
Are the noontime tables at Schrafft's and Stouffer's,
Are the maltless malteds that you go to Liggett's for,
The hit revues that you can't get tiggetts for,

The smog in the winter, the neon in the dark,
The avenues and avenues with nowhere to park,
The feel of the cinder, gritty on the pane,
And the hoot of the taxi as it passes in the rain.

Too new for an empire, too big for its boots,
With cold steel cables where it might have roots,
With everything to offer and nothing to give,
It's a horrid place to visit but a fine place to live;

For there's always the linen shop Selling Out Entire,
Always the parade and the three-alarm fire,
The strike on the buses, the scandal on the docks,
The ladies on their leashes that poodles take for walks,
The morning papers that you buy the night before,
And the riveter working on a ledge next door.

Ah! some love Paris,
And some Purdue.
But love is an archer with a low I. Q.
A bold, bad bowman, and innocent of pity.
So I'm in love with
New York City.

85 391